Mike's book is a gift to anyone who wants to take charge of their financial future. He clearly communicates these innovative yet safe financial concepts, making them accessible for each of us. All we, as readers, have to do is follow the breadcrumbs along the proven path Mike and others have already taken. Moreover, we don't have to go it alone! A safety net of supportive coaching is in place so that all of us can experience financial success. Getting closer!

—Chris Bay
Infinite Banking Coach

As a believer in the Infinite Banking Concept and the Income Snowball, I know that these concepts work. However, I also know that they can be difficult to fully understand. Mike's book explores these concepts and makes them easy to grasp. He explains them effortlessly and shows how you can make these concepts work for you.

—Toby Whitman

Mike is a wonderful human with an immense amount of passionate energy for helping others. This energy fueled his creative drive to combine Nelson Nash's Infinite Banking Concept and Tardus' Income Snowball strategy. With his in-depth understanding of these distinctive systems, Mike developed a reliable financial machine that can provide anyone—from the average household to the multimillionaire—with the means to reach their goals.

—Sharon Smith

AF697189

Providing financial stability for my family has long been a goal of mine, but I didn't think it was possible, especially on a teacher's salary. I am so thankful to Mike for introducing IBC to me, because now I can not only provide a financial legacy but also ensure my financial freedom. I recently started my second policy and know that I am able to pass something down to my three children and their families while still enjoying my retirement years. My son has started policies on himself and my grandson. My youngest daughter has also started her second policy and is just beginning her IBC journey.

—Evelyn Vohra

DIBS on Your Money!

The Dynamic Income Banking System, or DIBS, combines two unconventional money strategies to boost your cash flow and achieve true wealth and financial freedom.

MICHAEL KWONG, JD, MBA, EdM

DIBS on Your Money!
The Dynamic Income Banking System, or DIBS, combines two unconventional strategies to boost your cash flow and achieve true wealth and financial freedom.

Author: Michael Kwong, JD, MBA, EdM

Published by Tag Team Press, LLC
Copyright © 2022 by Michael Kwong, JD, MBA, EdM
All rights reserved.

No part of this publication may be reproduced, distributed, or transmitted in any form or by any means, including photocopying, recording, or other electronic or mechanical methods, without the prior written permission of the publisher, except in the case of brief quotations embodied in critical reviews and certain other noncommercial uses permitted by copyright law. For permission requests, write to the publisher, addressed "Attention: Permissions Coordinator," at the address below.

Tag Team Press, LLC
TagTeamPress@gmail.com

Limit of Liability/Disclaimer of Warranty:

While the publisher and author have used their best efforts in preparing this book, they make no representations or warranties with respect to the accuracy or completeness of the contents of this book and specifically disclaim any implied warranties of merchantability or fitness for a particular purpose. No warranty may be created or extended by sales representatives or written sales materials. Neither the publisher nor author shall be liable for any loss of profit or any other commercial damages, including but not limited to special, incidental, consequential, or other damages.

Publishing and editorial team:
Author Bridge Media, www.AuthorBridgeMedia.com
Editor: Helen Chang
Publishing Manager: Laurie Aranda

Library of Congress Control Number: 2022945783
ISBN: 979-8-9864292-0-5 – softcover
ISBN: 979-8-9864292-1-2 – ebook

Ordering Information:

Quantity sales. Special discounts are available on quantity purchases by corporations, associations, and others. For details, contact the publisher at the address above.

I dedicate this book to my dearest wife, Pei-Jiin, who stuck with me from the beginning of our journey—my unfailing strength and pillar of support throughout the ups and downs.

I wrote this for our beloved daughter, Jackie, who shall have it all one day and is my pride and inspiration to be a better man, father, and example to her and all who know me.

CONTENTS

Chapter 1

Introduction

In today's information age, we are flooded with data and ideas about money and what to do with it. Some are good and some not so good. How can we tell which is which? Should we invest in the stock market, with its historic ups and downs and persistent volatility? When is a good time to jump in (or out), and what stocks would I even buy? What about real estate? Is that the best asset class? After all, unless you're camping out under a bridge, pretty much everyone already lives in some sort of housing. But aren't the pundits and "Chicken Little" experts always talking about the bubble bursting, especially with rising interest rates?

What about cryptocurrency—or what I sometimes joke as digital "meme money" since, to be fair, some of them are named after internet dogs? All we need is a bullish tweet from Elon Musk and crypto goes through the roof, only to crash through the floor a few days later when Warren Buffett calls the currency a joke. For every crypto overnight millionaire, there are countless unheralded crypto crashers.

Each of these loudly touted asset classes inevitably suffers varying levels of uncertainty that leave someone like me, and maybe even you, feeling more than a little unsettled.

With record-setting inflation, steadily rising prices plaguing our roller-coaster economy, and its "bubblish," top-heavy stock and real estate markets ever ready to burst, what is one to do? Some people might throw their hands up in frustration and stuff their cash under the proverbial mattress and into their safe and secure bank accounts. But with increasing inflation far outpacing any nominal return we can hope to earn from simply saving, that's not only dead money you have there, but moreover, money that's rotting away in its purchasing power, day by day, year over year.

Given this state of affairs, wouldn't you want to learn about more productive things you can do with your money, rather than mere places to stash it and hope for the best? I mean *proven* strategies that not only bring your money to life, but also supercharge it to make more of it—even passively—all so it can flow and grow in a safe, secure manner that you can control and use, and even reuse, as you see fit and on your schedule. These strategies don't demand any change to your work or lifestyle and require only a bit of your time and effort to learn.

The Dynamic Income Banking System (DIBS) is what my brilliant wife, Pei-Jiin, and I discovered and have practiced over the years, drawn from our good and bad experiences of investing, doing business, and making money in all sorts of ways. It effectively combines the two most powerful financial strategies we know of and can provide you real financial security and consistent cash flow to match and even exceed your present income. DIBS can also set you up for early retirement and build a substantial legacy you can pass down to your next generation.

This book is for anyone. Whether you are just starting out as a young, single person with your first job, in the middle of your career and looking for a better way, or between jobs and just want to know more about finances and money, then this is for you. So long as you are willing to rethink with an open mind, this book can provide you a new and better way to take control of your finances, achieve whatever money goals you have in mind, and hopefully inspire you to rewrite them beyond what you thought was possible.

As parents, my wife and I strive to provide more for our daughter and a better lifestyle than we had growing up. I remember as a child immigrating from the Philippines with my family to this amazing country. We grew up pretty poor, financially speaking, but rich in the traditional Asian values my parents instilled in us, particularly pertaining to money, about being thrifty and respecting it. However, we lacked any real content, specific skills, or effective strategies to actually make more of this hard-earned money! Neither of my parents attended college, and because of that—especially being in a new country—they toiled long and hard for their entire working lives doing mostly manual labor.

My mom's first job in the US was at the local McDonald's in Vero Beach, FL, and my dad's was in a hot, greasy Chinese restaurant kitchen. Over the years, my mom has had jobs in retail, waited tables, cleaned houses, and even worked as a nurse's aide for a few years, cleaning up all sorts of other people's bodily functions and fluids. My dad started off as a cook and moved up to waiting tables, where the cash tips were at least better than the cook's meager pay, although he stayed in the restaurant business. They strongly encouraged my brother, sister, and me to use our brains, and not our backs, to work and make a living. In our parents' minds, getting into college would be the golden ticket to a better life.

I did make it into college, graduating from a shiny, expensive Ivy League university and from multiple graduate schools over the years. I took the term *lifelong learner* to a new level. In fact, as of today, in addition to my bachelor's degree and associate degree (which I happened to earn after my bachelor's), I have three graduate degrees: in law, business, and education. Believe it or not, I can count over twenty-three years of formal education under my belt over my lifetime!

Furthermore, I have worked in at least five different professions and industries since college. I started off in the fashion retail business in Boston as an assistant buyer; after law school, I worked in the legal field for a brief, miserable time. In order to learn Mandarin Chinese, originally to further my prospects in immigration law, I served in the Navy as a language analyst. My chosen rate was CTI, or cryptologic technician interpretive, so that I could attend the nation's top language school, the Defense Language Institute Foreign Language Center. That's where I nabbed that associate degree in Mandarin Chinese.

In exchange for that opportunity, I collected military intelligence for the National Security Agency (NSA). I had to admit that I never wanted to return to law. However, with my growing interest in business and finance, I eventually ended up in the insurance and financial realms. Here in Texas, I even taught for a few years at a public high school and elementary charter school after earning a master's degree in education (curriculum and instruction) on the Yellow Ribbon, Post-9/11 GI Bill Program.

My wife and I have also opened and run several businesses: a mom-and-pop, coin-operated laundromat in Massachusetts, a nationally established health and wellness MLM (multilevel-marketing) company, a credit repair service, and even a small bakery and purple dessert food truck named Lola, in Hawaii. All the while, we invested in residential real estate across all four states we've lived in, as far east as Massachusetts, where we met and married, and as far west as Hawaii, where our daughter, Jackie, was born.

Most recently, in the Houston area where we now live, we bought into and operated a nationwide college planning franchise for a couple of years, primarily to figure out how best to prepare our daughter for her eventual college application process. Over the more than two decades since we started it all, we made some good money and lost a bit too. However, we were generally always still working for our money, just like my parents before us had for all their lives. In time, though, that changed for us as we finally began to understand that it's far better to work smarter, not just harder—and also what that really means and just how to do it.

Chapter 2

The Purpose and Proper Mindset

My wife and I can provide more for our high schooler, Jackie, today than my parents ever could for me. In addition to the financial values of thrift and respect for money that my parents taught me, I want to empower Jackie with the proven money-making and management strategies that, over the years, we have learned and developed for her to implement for her own future and family. Unless someone is lucky enough to be a trust fund baby, most people work for their money, which is fine and certainly admirable in its own right. But they are often trading their precious time for that money, day in and day out, just to get their paychecks to make rent, pay bills, and move on with their busy lives.

Some people work so hard for their money that they inadvertently become slaves to it, almost never taking time off for themselves or their families. They are constantly running that rat race, faster and faster, or in a bigger or fancier wheel, with no real exit strategy or concrete means to get off it. However, you can break that cycle if you really want to. You simply need to learn how to flip the script and *make money work for you, instead of always working for it.* Unlike people, who can get sick, be fired, quit, take time off, go on vacation, or otherwise stop working or being productive, money never has to rest. It never complains and never has to stop growing, once you learn how to make it work for you.

Originally, my idea for this book sprung from a set of notes I was writing down for Jackie, who's now a teenager. Once I am physically gone and have "graduated off this earth," I want her to have an instruction manual or guidebook of sorts on how to best manage the money and assets we leave her. More importantly, even without those material things passed down to her, armed with the mindset, skills, and strategies in this book, she will be able to build her own self-perpetuating fortune, virtually from scratch. There's an old adage that goes, "You can give a person a fish, and she can eat but for a day. It's better to teach her *how to fish*, so she can feed herself forever." Ideally, that person will even have enough for others too.

I soon realized, though, that the knowledge gathered in this book, amassed over the years from our own real-life experiences of more than a few hard knocks, can really benefit anyone. With this strategy, my wife and I were able to leave our public school teaching jobs, close down and walk away from our college planning business, and be financially free and "job optional" by age forty-five. We now travel wherever and whenever we want to, with more than enough money coming in to enjoy it as well. In the midst of the global COVID-19 pandemic and resultant economic turmoil, this unique experience was particularly significant and worth sharing. So I decided to open up and write this book for anyone and everyone.

My sincere hope is that you not just "learn how to fish" or make your money work, but actually be able to fish and work those dollars in the most efficient manner possible. Whether in fishing or personal finance, it's not just about the gear or asset you choose, but more importantly, *the way you use and operate that gear or asset* if you want the very best results. For example, even if I had the most expensive set of clubs in the world, I am sure Tiger Woods, using nothing more than a hockey stick, would still embarrass me on the golf course! In a nutshell, the point is that *the practice and process is often more important than the product;* or put another way, *what you do is more important than what you have.* We will return to this theme later.

This book begins by challenging readers to question and redefine what real financial security means in order to have the proper mental context from which we will explore this topic. For example, when many people think of security, they may imagine an armored safe or an impregnable fortress that's heavy and set firmly in place. While this generally makes sense, this fixed and immobile stance is not always the best way to protect money, and certainly not ideal if you ever want it to thrive and increase.

For example, my favorite sport is boxing, and one of the finest technical boxers ever to lace up a pair of gloves was Floyd Mayweather Jr. His stunning, *Matrix*-level defense relied primarily on his catlike reflexes, fast feet, and fluid mobility. Hit and not be hit—that's the essence of what they call the sweet science of boxing. The last thing anyone wants to be is a sitting duck! My point is that agility and flexibility in both body and mind are important traits to develop, whether you are boxing, working, or, especially, dealing with your finances.

To that end, this book shifts us from the traditional, static, and somewhat problematic **accumulation model** and way of thinking toward the more progressive, dynamic, and useful **cash-flow model** and mindset. It illuminates an age-old money mechanism and set of universal forces and principles that's ever at work in the financial world. It describes and explains the two powerful systems of the **Infinite Banking Concept** (IBC) financial strategy and the **Income Snowball** that harness and synergize these dynamics to work in your favor, both immediately and for the long term. And it concludes by explaining why and how, through DIBS, you can run them together for maximum efficiency and financial benefit.

Ultimately, the effective implementation of DIBS will have you running your Income Snowball within your IBC banking system to provide consistent, increasing passive income and accumulate significant wealth over time for you and your family. It's not just more money that these systems will bring you and your family, but more importantly, the freedom from the financial and time constraints that often hold people back. In short, imagine how you will be able to fulfill your true purpose or follow your life's passions, without the common worries of having enough money to live and pass on to your loved ones.

Chapter 3

YOUR HOUSE OF MONEY AND CASH FLOW

I liken the systems in this book to the building of a house of money and financial security. First, you must be educated and know how construction works to even begin building. To this end, we examine the mighty banking business and institution to understand how it really functions and how you can harness its principles and power for your own benefit. Next, we can "clear the lot" that you'll be building upon, which, financially speaking for many folks, means paying off and clearing out consumer debt using the fastest and most efficient means of debt elimination. If you are one of them, then you'll want to learn all about **Velocity Banking**. This is a personal finance approach that uses a home equity line of credit (HELOC) or similar revolving credit account to leverage with your disposable income to pay down your primary mortgage or any expensive consumer debt while saving on the amortized interest.

Now you can start constructing your financial house by first laying down a solid foundation upon which you build your frame, walls, roof, and such. The IBC financial strategy is your bedrock financial foundation and forms your base from which to best operate. This is the practice of being your own banker by using a system of high-cash-value whole life insurance policies to enjoy uninterrupted compounding growth, guaranteed and tax free, all while financing for yourself everything you need and even want in your life. With IBC, you essentially have your own private banking system where your cash flow operates in an optimal financial environment that you alone control and benefit from. Your banking system provides your house of wealth a base foundation, solid framework, and protective roof of tremendous strength, security in its guarantees, and even flexibility to proceed safely with whatever ventures you decide to invest in or adventures you wish to embark upon.

Once your IBC foundation is in place, you can put up the rest of the house and install windows and the proper wiring and piping to ensure that your house can let in light, circulate air, and run electricity and water easily, safely, and in the most efficient manner. This is essentially the application of the same Velocity Banking concepts we used to pay off debts and run our IBC, but now reengineered to create and begin amassing your Income Snowball. This proven and systematized method of investing in amortized, long-term, income-producing assets uses leverage or other people's money like a HELOC or personal line of credit, providing you steady monthly and even increasing income for life.

But first, let's get our heads into the right state of mind. Like Robert Kiyosaki, author of *Rich Dad Poor Dad*, says, all the content in the world is worthless without the proper context and right mindset through which to receive it.

Ben Franklin is often attributed to saying, "A penny saved is a penny earned." Although not historically accurate, the popular sentiment remains. For many, this means that you should save as much money as you can, so you can build up a "nest egg" for retirement in the future. This accumulation model is the prevailing philosophy of personal finance we are all typically taught to operate under, the major assumption being that by doing so, after working so many years you should have saved up enough money to live off of at retirement. Eventually, you can finally crack open that nest egg and feed off of it for the rest of your life, ideally with a little extra to pass onto your kids, grandkids, and/or favorite cause or charity.

At retirement, you begin regularly withdrawing from your ideally substantially sized bundle and hope that it lasts—at least as long as you do. In fact, under this savings-oriented accumulation model, what you ultimately want is for your money to outlive you. Or to put it more morbidly, you want to die before your money does! But just how much money will you need to save up? This figure naturally depends on how long you plan to live. Of course, for the vast majority of us, this is a best-guess estimate and not often pleasant to ponder either.

One popular exercise to help you figure out your target nest egg number uses what's called the Monte Carlo simulation. It's a fairly simple mathematical formula where you reverse-engineer a targeted result by calculating in a set of inputs that you determine first. Assuming that you plan to retire at sixty-five and die at ninety, we typically apply a safe withdrawal amount of 4 percent per year to pay out from your nest egg and live off of, for up to twenty-five years or age ninety, before it's all gone. Depending on how conservative you want to be, this annual withdrawal percentage can be adjusted down to last you longer or up in case you want your golden years to be a bit more platinum-plated. But for this example, we will use 4 percent.

First, determine how much you need to live on *per month* to pay all your bills (shelter, food, clothing, travel, entertainment, medicine, etc.). Let's say that figure is $5,000 per month. Next, *multiply* that by twelve for an annual requirement, which comes out neatly to $60,000 per year. Now, here's the fun part: *divide* that $60,000 by your 4 percent annual draw and—voilà!—you have your magic nest-egg requirement of $1.5 million!

Wait, what? You'll need to have a million-and-a-half in the bank to retire comfortably! Finally, consider this truly sobering thought: Just how long would someone who can reliably put away even $1,000 per month need to save to reach that magical $1.5 million number? Quick math shows that it would take fifteen *hundred* months, or one hundred twenty-five *years*!

Fortunately, there's a better and more useful way to consider and solve this rather disconcerting situation. I call it the cash-flow model and mindset. Instead of dwelling on the daunting task of saving up a nest egg of a million and a half that will take over a century to amass, you simply figure what your monthly expenses are to see how much passive, perpetual income you'll need to live comfortably on, and then focus on that goal. Recall that $5,000 per month figure earlier. This much smaller number is easier to manage and achieve than trying to hoard the $1.5 million we needed before.

The biggest difference here is that the *cash-flow model is focused on the present and persistent production of monthly, passive income.* This mindset shifts us from what the accumulation model is fixated on, which is merely saving up money to be stored and sitting idly in the bank or in your retirement fund until you hit sixty-five or somehow achieve that magical $1.5 million value. Also, in my opinion, the cash-flow model can be a lot more fun and rewarding way of looking at things and living life than merely counting your pennies and drudgingly stashing them away like Scrooge McDuck.

Chapter 4

RICH VS. WEALTHY AND THE FOX IN THE CHICKEN COOP

Another important distinction that we sometimes take for granted—but that I want to stress—is the difference in what it means to be *rich* versus *wealthy*. For most folks, these words are synonyms and, thus, interchangeable. Both sound good, after all, and certainly much better than being poor or financially insecure. However, while being rich generally means that you make lots of money or have a significant income, both of which are measured in dollars, wealth is more nuanced. You see, being wealthy is not just a function of an amount of money, but better measured in the *time* one enjoys with that abundance of money.

For example, a rich person may make a lot of money but also have high expenses and large bills. If the person stopped working, at some point they could no longer enjoy the lifestyle they are accustomed to, since the money goes in and (for many, at least) right back out again. Think of the old saying "keeping up with the Joneses." Each promotion comes with a bigger car, boat, or house, and then private school for the kids and, of course, college too. But wait, you can always cut back on your expenses and just live within your means, right? Frankly, in the present record-breaking inflationary economic environment we're in, that option doesn't seem too realistic, and certainly no fun.

Wealth, on the other hand, is measured in how long, or how many months or even years, that you can continue living your lifestyle *without working*. Of course, having a big salary helps, but the focus here is really about *time freedom*. Think about it: if a person, even if they are rich, suddenly lost their job or their source of income earned from working in or running a business, how long could they really continue to live as they did before? Sure, there may be unemployment benefits for a time, or some savings to hold them over, but eventually, most people will need to find something new and get back to work.

A wealthy person is a different animal altogether.

Simply put, a truly wealthy person could go on indefinitely and doesn't have to go to work—not now, and not for the rest of their lives. Remember that everyone, whether rich or poor, and of course the wealthy too, has a minimum monthly dollar amount of expenses and bills they must pay to live on or support their families. This number often fluctuates and generally increases each year. Whatever that amount is, *a wealthy person has at least that much—typically much more, in fact—coming in every month, and moreover, it typically comes in* passively, *whether they get up in the morning or not.*

This is the key difference between the two states of financial wellness, between being merely rich and being truly wealthy. It's not a dollar amount, per se, but rather lies in the *nature* of one's cash flow. Instead of someone perpetually working for and actively earning their money, the money works *for* the truly wealthy folks. Best of all, with some time, interest, and effort, pretty much anyone can learn how to become wealthy within their lifetime, as my own life example and this book will prove to you, hopefully.

I remember being taught as a child to do well in school, earn good grades, go to college, find a good job, and then simply work and save, work and save, until retirement, so we could eventually live out our golden years in comfort. What was touted as the "American Dream" over the years I have come to realize as something quite different. I now call this the "40/40/40 Deal." You know: you work forty hours a week for forty years, and then hope to retire on just 40 percent of your prior working income. This is between what you've saved up in your nest egg and the pittance they call social security, which is, in my opinion, really the biggest legalized Ponzi scheme ever. Run by the federal government, the system, as it stands, mathematically cannot sustain itself for much longer. I don't know about you, but I am not exactly thrilled to sign up for that bargain—not that we have much of a choice, since the government automatically takes 6.2 percent (as of this writing, at least) of your earnings as your social security payment into the system.

Even worse, in reality, the 40/40/40 Deal isn't even that ideal. For example, most people work far beyond forty hours per week, especially if you include commuting time, working from home, extra hours, and overtime, etc. And if you start working at age twenty (I got my first job at sixteen while still in high school), precious few folks actually retire after forty years at age sixty, as the current set retirement age is sixty-five, and more and more seniors are working well into their seventies just to pay their bills. Somehow we have been duped into believing that running along this vicious, never-ending hamster wheel is the dream rather than the nightmare that many discover too late in life.

Finally, in today's modern world, convenience is king, and to that end, sometimes it's more convenient to have just a few choices or decisions to make, or better yet, to be able to delegate responsibility to someone else to worry about. It's no different in the financial world, where you can just "search up" (as my daughter and her friends say), google the top-performing mutual funds to buy, or even hire a foxy financial planner to manage your money, who will often just do the same, picking his or her own fund or stock mix to invest your hard-earned money into.

Don't get me wrong: delegating this responsibility to someone else is easy and fairly simple. But no one cares more about your hard-earned money than you do, right? And guess who gets paid, no matter how your portfolio or fund performs, based on the various and often hidden commissions and fees that will eat into any profit you might be lucky enough to eke out? You got it—that same slick money manager with the fluffy tail! Somehow this reminds me of leaving the fox to tend to your nest-egg-laying chickens!

Let's get started and go beyond simply caring about your money and move toward being a more responsible, effective, and self-directed manager of your own capital and financial future.

Chapter 5

The Big Problem: Debt

"I owe . . . I owe . . . so off to work I go!"

When trying to get ahead, we typically focus on the forward momentum or, in the case of money, the positive rate of return we can squeeze out from our investments. No doubt, such a positive return on investment (ROI) can certainly help, but for every 5–10 percent increase we can improve upon, a much larger and more consequential factor that most people never even consider is almost always at play. This looming monster can hold them back far more than any modest increase in ROI can ever help them. What could this be? Debt! Specifically, we are talking about all the interest fees this debt costs us every month and year, which we all too often ignore. This negative drag or headwind of debt must be dealt with, and paid off, before any appreciable gains in your investments can make a real difference to your bottom line.

According to the Federal Reserve, the total American household debt hit a record $14.6 *trillion* in the spring of 2021, with the average American being $90,460 in debt, according to a 2021 CNBC report. Like a leaking bathtub, your pool of money will be constantly depleted, whether in the form of taxes to the government or interest to the banks, and you will be facing a constant uphill battle. Any meager single-digit gains from your savings, CDs (certificates of deposit), or money-market accounts will be eaten up by this negative, often double-digit drag. Therefore, it makes sense that one of your first and fundamental tasks to improve your financial situation would be to pay down your debts as fast as possible to save on all that interest leaking out every month.

Conventional wisdom and many financial entertainers advise you to pay any extra dollars you earn toward the credit card balances, car/student loans, and/or mortgage to squash this debt and reduce the overall interest expenses they incur. To that end, it seems rather sensible that we should attack the highest-interest-rate debt first, right? This assumption, however, overlooks other key factors you must consider if you want the best and fastest way to eliminate debt. Besides the annual percentage rate (APR) of interest charged, you should also identify the *nature* of each debt, which determines *how* that interest is charged to you. Is the debt *revolving*, or are *payments fixed*? Is the interest accrued daily and *simple* (good and generally cheaper), or is it *amortized* and/or *compounded* over many years, which is bad and typically more expensive? (unless you're earning it!)

Chapter 6

THE NATURE VS. JUST THE NUMBERS

A debt can often be in the form of a loan with a fixed-interest rate that you pay off over a set number of years, maybe five years for a car note or thirty years for a home mortgage. When so structured, it is considered *amortized* for the lifetime of the loan, which is just a fancy way of saying you pay it off over time with regular monthly payments. Although the advertised APR may be low, what you end up paying in interest is often much more than you might expect. Why? Because the lenders precalculate your interest according to the *entire expected lifetime* of the loan, and you are charged the full five years of interest for the car note or the thirty years of interest for the house mortgage. Furthermore, this interest is charged up front, and then all split up over the scheduled sixty or three hundred sixty monthly payments. The plus side is that because the lenders stretched out the loan schedule, each month's payment amount is really quite low. But this is where unsuspecting borrowers are lulled into this sweet "deal," since it now magically fits into their monthly budget!

Let's look at a typical mortgage for a $400,000 house that you bought with a 20 percent down payment ($80,000) and a thirty-year mortgage with a 5 percent APR. After that hefty down payment, you are immediately subject to a fixed repayment schedule of $1,717.83 every month, to be paid like clockwork. This, of course, doesn't include property taxes and home insurance, which often adds several hundred more to that figure. But hold on—this is just the beginning!

Take a close look at the table below. It lays out your annual payments toward your mortgage for the thirty years and breaks down each year's payment into the principal paid down and the interest paid out to the bank. Make sure you have a seat, take a deep breath, and let's start with year one:

Year	Interest	Principal	Total	LTV	Balance
2021	15,892.78	4,721.17	20,613.95	78.8	315,278.83
2022	15,651.24	4,962.71	20,613.95	77.6	310,316.12
2023	15,397.34	5,216.61	20,613.95	76.3	305,099.50
2024	15,130.44	5,483.51	20,613.95	74.9	299,616.00
2025	14,849.90	5,764.05	20,613.95	73.5	293,851.94
2026	14,555.00	6,058.95	20,613.95	71.9	287,792.99

Notice that your twelve monthly payments total $20,613.95, in the fourth column, for the first year and each year thereafter. Well, since the rate is 5 percent, doing some quick math, you must be paying just over $1,000 for interest, right? After all, that's 5 percent of $20,000 and would seem to make sense . . . but slow down, sailor! Look closely at the red column of interest actually paid, there in the second column: **$15,892.78!** Take that number and divide it into your annual payment of $20,613.95, and you'll soon see that you really end up *paying 77 percent in interest for that first year alone*! Nor does your situation improve much next year or the year after (75.9 percent and 74.7 percent, respectively).

Year	Interest	Principal	Total	LTV	Balance
2021	15,892.78	4,721.17	20,613.95	78.8	315,278.83
2022	15,651.24	4,962.71	20,613.95	77.6	310,316.12
2023	15,397.34	5,216.61	20,613.95	76.3	305,099.50
2024	15,130.44	5,483.51	20,613.95	74.9	299,616.00
2025	14,849.90	5,764.05	20,613.95	73.5	293,851.94
2026	14,555.00	6,058.95	20,613.95	71.9	287,792.99
2027	14,245.01	6,368.94	20,613.95	70.4	281,424.05
2028	13,919.16	6,694.79	20,613.95	68.7	274,729.26
2029	13,576.64	7,037.31	20,613.95	66.9	267,691.95
2030	13,216.60	7,397.35	20,613.95	65.1	260,294.61
2031	12,838.14	7,775.81	20,613.95	63.1	252,518.80
2032	12,440.31	8,173.64	20,613.95	61.1	244,345.16
2033	12,022.14	8,591.81	20,613.95	58.9	235,753.35
2034	11,582.56	9,031.39	20,613.95	56.7	226,721.96
2035	11,120.50	9,493.45	20,613.95	54.3	217,228.51
2036	10,634.80	9,979.15	20,613.95	51.8	207,249.35
2037	10,124.24	10,489.71	20,613.95	49.2	196,759.65
2038	9,587.57	11,026.38	[illegible]	[illegible]	185,733.27
2039	9,023.44	11,590.51	[illegible]	[illegible]	174,142.76
2040	8,430.45	12,183.50	[illegible]	[illegible]	161,959.26
2041	7,807.12	12,806.83	20,613.95	37.3	149,152.42

$350,437.15

But wait, it gets better. Well, for the bank at least—not so much for you. Run quite a bit further down the schedule, and you'll notice that you don't actually "break even" as far as your interest-to-principal ratio, where it's at or below 50 percent of your monthly payment, until year 2037. That's seventeen long years of paying more than 50 percent interest to the bank. Also, if you add up all those payments over the years, you'd see that you have sunk over $350,000 into that $320,000 mortgage, quite a bit more than the original mortgage itself, and yet you still owe the bank $196,759.65! Does this make sense to you? It sure does for the bank. Behold the awesome power of amortized interest!

The next graph colorfully illustrates for our visual learners the tremendous, front-loaded skew that the banks build into mortgages to ensure that they get as much of their interest back as soon as possible. With the red portion as interest and the blue as principal, you can see that the point when the red and blue sections eventually cross (and thus are equal) is just after that aforementioned year, 2037, when the interest amount finally drops below your slowly rising principal amount.

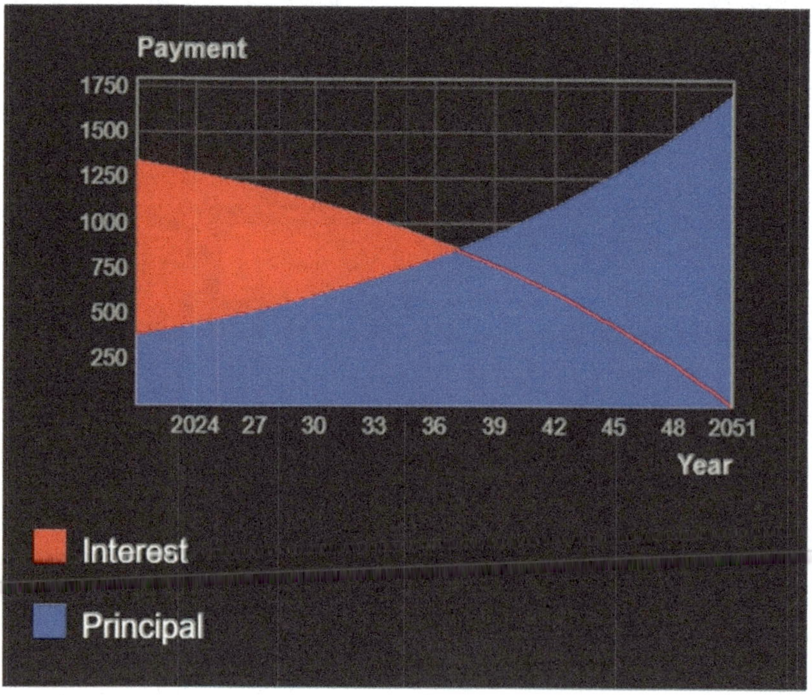

Thankfully, there is another kind of debt, known as revolving, such as that found in—surprisingly—a credit card or, better yet, a line of credit. Although these typically have a higher APR, in the end they can actually be cheaper for you than the amortized debt with the lower rates. What kind of malarkey is this? Again, the answer lies in the *nature* of the interest and how it is calculated.

Revolving debt charges you interest based on whatever the current balance is at the time, unlike amortized debt, which is fixed up front and based on the original, highest amount. Furthermore, revolving debt is figured on a daily basis, so if you have the money out for, say, only six days, you pay the interest accrued for only those six days. As a note, in the particular case of a credit card, that interest charge doesn't even start until after your payment cycle ends, thus affording you up to a month of interest-free float. In other words, as long as you make your full payment on your credit card for that billing cycle, you won't be charged a penny in interest.

Let's take an initial balance of $10,000 in such a revolving account. The interest rate is 8 percent APR (calculated annually). Quick math would have you expect to pay $800 for interest on such a debt. However, if you pay it off in a month, you pay only about $66, or $2.20 per day. Simply take the $800 (which it would cost for the entire year, as APR is calculated) and divide that by 365 for the daily rate. Now multiply that daily rate by the number of days you have the balance out, and you will almost always end up paying a much lower overall amount in interest.

Even if you don't pay off the entire balance at once, but rather break it up and pay it down over so many months, each time you do so decreases the running balance upon which they calculate the interest they charge you. For example, if you simply paid it down bit by bit each month over the year, your monthly payment is $868.59, and your total interest comes out to just $423.13. Out of the original $10,000 borrowed, that represents just 4.23 percent interest, much less than the 8 percent, or $800, you expected to pay. The takeaway here is that *the nature of the debt is more important than the mere number of the debt's interest rate.*

Chapter 7

ENTER VELOCITY BANKING: THE SWISS ARMY KNIFE OF FINANCE

Now that we're enlightened and armed with these important truths about debt and interest, how can we use this knowledge to help us? Velocity Banking is a personal finance strategy that takes advantage of these critical features of debt and leverage to allow you to do incredible things with your money and cash flow. Originally, it gained fame for its ability to help you quickly knock out debt by using and leveraging OPM (other people's money). In this case, you use a commercial bank's money via a revolving line of credit (LOC) to pay off high-interest consumer debts and/or your amortized mortgage much faster. This saves you lots of interest—much more than if you just paid down your debt directly with the money you earn each month.

Remember that not all debt is created equal. Interest rates can be a handy way to compare your debts. But that's just one measure among other considerations. What is your debt's remaining balance? What is your monthly payment? For Velocity Banking, you determine the efficiency of each debt to prioritize them and pay each down accordingly. Really, this is the measure of how much "bang for your buck" paying off each debt means to you in terms of how much it costs you to service that debt monthly, and how much money you would free up when the debt is paid off so that you can, in turn, add that amount to your positive cash flow or continue debt paydown.

Let's compare two debts: a revolving one on a credit card versus a fixed one for a car loan. The credit card has a 12 percent APR with a $150 minimum monthly payment and a remaining balance of $4,000. The car loan has a much lower 5 percent APR but a $300/month payment and a balance of $5,000. I bet your "spidey sense" is tingling: "Pay off the credit card first, *duh*!" But let's crunch it out to compare their actual relative efficiency.

The first step is to take each remaining balance and divide it by the monthly payment to get you an efficiency score. The higher the score, the more efficient the debt, whereas the lower the score, the less efficient it is. The credit card debt's calculation is $4,000 / $150 = **26.67**. The car loan is $5,000 / $300 = **16.67**. The car loan's score is lower and *less efficient* and therefore takes priority. You see, despite the lower APR, it behooves you to pay the car off first. Why? Because ultimately, this will free up more of your money to pay off the rest of your debts faster, or, on the flip side, begin working for you and earning more interest earlier. The lesson here: *pay off your most inefficient debts first, in descending order.*

Okay, so through the first step to Velocity Banking you have properly prioritized your debts and know in which order to pay them off, and now you can simply redirect every extra dollar of your income toward the worst first and pay them all down in that order, right? To be honest, this is just half the story. In fact, an even faster way to do this, rather than using your own hard-earned money to pay down your debt, is the second key part to Velocity Banking: *to leverage other people's money* to do the very same thing. This will really turbocharge your debt paydown.

How does—and why would—Velocity Banking have you use someone else's money to pay off debts through a revolving LOC rather than directly from your own income or savings? After all, weren't we taught that debt is bad, and owing anyone anything is a big no-no? Actually, borrowing money sometimes can be beneficial and is more than worth the cost of it, especially if you don't have your own immediately available, but sometimes even if you *do* have your own to use. This makes sense only if *the input value (or cost required) for the production of a favorable result is much less than the output value or savings/profit gained from that result.* Simply put, when using OPM is done right, you get more out of it than you paid for it.

In physics, we use advantageous angles and levers or pulleys to create what is known as mechanical "leverage." In the financial world, more specifically for Velocity Banking purposes, leverage is the strategic use of OPM at *differing rates* and for *varying time frames.* Again, if you could use other people's money to pay off your debt and save much more in the end than it costs to do so, then aren't you better off for it? In particular, you can use an LOC from a bank or another similarly low/simple interest financing instrument *for a short time* to pull money out to *quickly extinguish* more *costly, high-interest, longer-term* debt.

Two critical factors are at play here. Number one, you're using cheaper money to pay off more expensive money. This is easy to grasp, like when you consolidate two or more high-interest credit card debts into one lower-interest note to pay less interest overall. But what's deeper and even more powerful is the 1) *nature* of and 2) *time value* element in this process.

First, note that the new borrowed money you use to pay off the debt is charged interest on a *daily basis*, and when used just briefly, only costs a little. However, the debt that you're paying off accrues interest very differently and *is calculated based on the much longer duration* of the loan or note in mind. Maybe it's a five-year car note or that horrendous thirty-year mortgage! Remember, lenders *amortize* payments and interest over that long (and thus expensive) time period so they can take their interest first and then apply your principal last, which, in the end, is much more costly for you.

The other piece to Velocity Banking relates to what you do with the money that was going toward the debt you just paid off. Now without that monthly payment, you should redirect those additional "freed up" dollars toward paying off the next most inefficient debt. This will more quickly extinguish the second debt account and free up several more dollars to combine with your current ones to attack the next debt. This has a real cascade effect; just rinse and repeat the process as this adds increasing "velocity" to your war on debt. This strategy does not require any extra income to work, since it's specifically designed for your existing cash-flow levels and payment schedule. It's really just a matter of reprioritizing your debts and redirecting your cash flows each and every month to annihilate your total debt burden in the fastest means possible.

Let's get back to that mortgage we broke down on the

$400,000 house for which we, for seventeen painful years, paid more to interest than to principal. Why is this particular financial instrument engineered so unfavorably against the borrower? (Hint: because it's great for the lender banks!) For one thing, this is *compound interest* at work *against you*, in its most treacherous form, amortized over a thirty-year time frame. The bank wants its money back as soon as possible, with you paying much of that interest up front. This is simply how home mortgages are designed, completely in the banks' interest, and "*to the banks, as interest.*"

Now, given this already sorry state of affairs, what do most people usually do after five to seven years? By then, many families have one or more children and need more space or a better school district or want newer digs since their income has also likely increased. They go back onto the market and upgrade to a new house with a new mortgage! Unbeknownst to them, this totally resets that bank-biased thirty-year mortgage clock, and the whole sham restarts once more, again with the borrower at the losing end of the bargain.

What else often happens? People may choose to stay in their house, but then see or look for a "better rate" and decide to refinance the entire mortgage. What this does is take your (hopefully smaller) remaining balance and makes a brand new thirty-year mortgage, but with a new (lower) rate. Naturally, this lowers your monthly payment and lulls the borrower into the fallacy of being in a better situation. It all sounds good, right? Consider the fact that the bank already got a major portion of your interest paid out to them from the original mortgage. Furthermore, how many people do you know will have the discipline of refusing the attractive cash-out option of the equity portion of your house? Not many. (Even I have been guilty of it.) Now, with the new mortgage (and similarly high interest-to-principal ratioed gearing), the bank will again enjoy a majority of that interest up front as before, and you, the borrower, are happily paying them that over time, for even more years to come.

What on earth can we do to avoid or improve this sad situation? The revolutionary idea is again based on shifting the long-term, compounded interest debt (the most expensive kind) onto a simple interest vehicle for the short term (much cheaper money). At the same time, through what is known as "chunking" the debt, you take lump sums of cash saved up (or better yet, freed up and/or gained for use) to pay down the mortgage and accelerate your mortgage schedule, shaving off thousands of dollars in interest and speeding up your payoff date.

Surprisingly, the most efficient and powerful way to do this is through using other people's money. That's right; you borrow it. However, now we'll take it to the next level and see that you don't just borrow from any old commercial bank, which controls all the terms of your loan, but from *your own bank* of capital that you control and benefit directly from. By doing so, rather than *paying* that expensive *compounding interest*, you can now *earn* that compounding interest, because it's *your* bank!

Chapter 8

The Infinite Banking Concept: Be Your Own Banker!

It's been said that banking is the most important business in a civilized society. Whether you agree or not, it's undeniably one of the most profitable. Interestingly, the banks themselves do not make any valuable goods, like the food we eat or the clothes we wear. Nor do banks provide handy services, like the local garage does when it changes my car's oil and fixes my brakes. Essentially, all banks do is move money around and around. It goes from you to them (in the form of deposits), and then out to others and even back to you (in the form of loans). Serving this vital function, banks are the pumps for the oil (think of money as flowing currency) in the smooth-running engine of our economies, whether locally, nationally, or globally. Without banks, money could not flow like it does, and businesses could not operate or even start up in many cases.

But what if I simply deposit my money and leave it "in the bank" to save up for my nest egg, or just stash it there until next year when I withdraw it to buy that shiny new car? Isn't my money just sitting there the whole time, waiting for me? Not a chance! Through an obscure but amazing financial practice known as *fractional reserve banking*, banks are allowed to take every dollar in deposit from you and me and turn around and lend it back out into the market, up to nine or ten times that amount, in the form of home mortgages, car notes, business or personal loans, etc. For example, say you deposited $100 into your savings account. Since by law banks are only required to keep as little as 10 percent of their outstanding loans on reserve as deposits, this means that they can now lend up to $1,000 in new, interest-earning loans to the rest of us! So they pay you for the $100 you have with them, and they now get to make more money with up to $1,000 that they, in turn, can lend out to the public.

Furthermore, for the 0.01 percent annual percentage yield (APY) they pay you in interest for your deposit within your savings account, the banks get to lend this money at anywhere from three to twelve hundred times as much (3–12 percent versus 0.01percent . . . you do the math!). In sum, not only are they earning a *lot* more interest dollar for dollar than they pay you to use *your* money, but they are earning significantly extra interest on effectively "imaginary" dollars as well, many times what you, me, or anyone else ever actually deposits. This is the institutional application of multiple uses and exponential leveraging of each dollar. To me, that's nothing short of financial wizardry—or witchcraft, depending on which side of that financial process (or scheme) you happen to be on.

How does the IBC financial strategy fit into all of this? A spry, southern gentleman by the name of R. Nelson Nash recognized this powerful banking phenomenon and developed this ingenious self-banking system and practice for our own use as private citizens. Simply put, IBC allows you and your family and/or business to set up your own private banking system so you can "be your own banker" and recapture all that interest expense that normally flows out of our hands to the banks. Additionally, through this private, controlled, and self-sustaining cash-flow control system, you not only save yourself from paying out interest, but also get to essentially earn it in the form of dividends. Your own money pool grows perpetually and, as a storehouse for your wealth, it becomes even more and more efficient—for life. When properly engineered, your system's growth and wealth compounds uninterrupted, and even completely tax-free, as long as specific rules and limits are followed.

Just how does the IBC financial strategy work for us everyday folks? This is not some newfangled, theoretical product or concept dreamed up by some exotic, far-away treasury official or royal prince with a surprise windfall to share with you online. The key lies with an age-old, time-tested, financial contract: the *dividend-paying whole life insurance policy from a mutual insurance company*. You might be surprised to learn that the very concept and practice of life insurance has been around for centuries, even millennia, at least since the ancient Greeks and Romans created guilds called "benevolent societies" as early as 600 BC. These provided for the families of deceased members and even paid for funeral expenses.

Today, of course, we have incorporated and contractualized

this agreement in the form of life insurance companies and their traditional whole life policies. To properly set up your IBC system, however, you must open a *dividend-paying whole life policy from a financially solid mutual life insurance company.* Mutual just means that these companies are privately held and, thus, not beholden to outside shareholders (as public companies are), who would normally receive the profits earned in the form of dividends paid. Instead, mutual life companies pay their dividends back to the policyholders themselves, who effectively *are* the partial or "mutual" owners of the company, and therefore are exclusively privy to the profits. That's right: you and I, as whole life policyholders, *are*, in effect, the owners of the mutual insurance company.

These annual dividends can be paid out in cash or, better yet, elected to be reinvested right back into your policy (as IBC would recommend). When so done, the dividend money purchases what's known as paid-up additions (PUA), which buys you additional insurance, both death benefit and cash value, at no cost to you. Furthermore, as your policy grows each year, it can even become *self-sustaining*, in that the dividends will first match and then, in time, even exceed the annual premium payment required (which is guaranteed never to increase) to keep the policy in force. At that point, you can simply elect to have the dividend pay for your premiums and thus never need to pay another dime! An IBC policy structured with this PUA option, known in insurance terms as a PUA rider, allows you to deposit extra money each year into your policy well beyond your base premium to enjoy this boosted growth, which compounds year over year.

Another powerful advantage of these private policies is the

significant tax benefit that they enjoy. To date, and ever since they started, the growth in such whole life insurance policies is not taxed and remains that way as long as they do not exceed what's known as the modified endowment contract (MEC) limit. This rule merely restricts how much PUA one can overfund their policies each year before it becomes a taxable event. IBC recommends funding up your policy with additional PUA as close to that limit as possible, without going over it.

The proper application of IBC also recommends a very select number of the highest-rated and financially strong mutual insurance companies, all sporting at least A, if not double or triple A or A+ credit ratings. Most of these mutual life insurance companies are over one hundred years old, even predating the Social Security Administration (SSA), which was enacted in 1935. In fact, a few even predate the establishment of the Internal Revenue Service (IRS), which was founded in 1862! Besides their considerable longevity, these mutual companies also boast solid histories of financial solvency, as evidenced by them paying dividends year after year, even during the two world wars, the Great Depression, and through every bust the economy has suffered in the past century.

How exactly does a life insurance policy allow me to Be the Banker and enjoy all of these benefits? For starters, the life insurance contract is not considered an "investment" per se, and therefore is not under the scope of the IRS or Securities and Exchange Commission (SEC) for income taxation or securities regulation purposes. Rather, it's a private contractual agreement between you, as the policyholder/owner, often as the insured (but not necessarily, as you can insure your children or business partners too), and the life insurance company, as the insurer. You simply arrange to make fixed, periodic premium payments to support the death benefit that is guaranteed to you, or rather to your beneficiaries upon your passing.

This regular schedule of premium payments is guaranteed fixed, from the first year's payment to the maturity date of the policy, which is technically when the policy is "paid off" and typically structured to be at the insured's expected attained age of somewhere between seventy-five and one hundred twenty, depending on the company and particular whole life product. At this point, the policy vests and is guaranteed to pay out the stipulated death benefit, sometimes even to the actual insured person, if he/she is lucky enough to still be alive!

With an IBC-styled policy and the proper practice of it, due to the many years of reinvested dividends and compounding growth, the death benefit grows at an ever-increasing rate until it is paid out, upon either your passing or your reaching that stipulated age of maturity (whichever comes first). Note also that the death benefit amount at any point generally far exceeds the total amount ever paid into the policy, typically considered your cost basis, per se. Not a bad deal at all, I would argue . . . but this is where most people's understanding of the whole life policy ends.

Chapter 9

IBC Is All about That Cash Value

The paramount feature of a properly structured, IBC-oriented, dividend-paying whole life policy lies in the guaranteed cash value that accumulates within it from the first year on and over its entire life. Think of this as an internal savings account (or maybe equity, like a mortgage has) within the policy that grows and grows as you pay your premiums and reinvest your annual dividends. Driving this growth, remember, is the addition of your PUA rider. This provision allows a policyowner to purchase additional insurance without additional medical underwriting, at no cost, and typically at any time. For IBC purposes, we want this extra cash option front-loaded at the onset of any policy to get that full (up to MEC) capitalization and compounding momentum started sooner than later.

Already great in its own right, a whole life policy additionally allows you to act like the banks do and borrow from, or more specifically, *take out loans* ***against***, the currently available cash value, which is simply collateralized by the death benefit. Note, I did not say withdraw or take money out of the policy, which would only serve to interrupt and stunt the compounding growth. By borrowing it out, you essentially get to use the money in your policy's cash values, but with a distinct twist that banks do not permit.

Rather than paying interest out (and gone forever) to a bank, the interest on your policy loans is paid back directly to *your life insurance company* as a stable income source for them, and then indirectly back to your own policy in the form of the dividend at year-end. Doing so necessarily increases your cash value and death benefit. This clearly benefits you, as the owner of the entity and the entire banking process. Furthermore, *by borrowing AGAINST it, you get to use it a second time, concurrently, and thus never interrupt the first instance of it as it grows and compounds over time.* This last sentence is worth reading again and again, until the full weight of this incredible benefit to you really sinks in.

Most people easily see the benefit of using your own cash value to borrow from and finance your purchases, at least as compared to borrowing from some outside bank's capital. But what if you do have enough of your own money to pay for whatever you want to buy, spend on, or invest in? Some people at this point invariably conclude: "*Why should I ever borrow money at all, if I can pay for it myself, with ready cash on hand, and not have to pay any interest on it?*" This one may be a tougher concept for most to grasp, but let us now consider the retail rewards-card analogy that follows.

Say you want to buy the latest MacBook laptop that you see on sale at Best Buy for $2,000. Well lucky you, you happen to have $3,000 in your savings account burning a hole in your proverbial wallet and smugly say to yourself, *"I'll just take out the $2,000 and buy it outright. No interest, no problem, right?"* Well, hold on a second. Let's also say that you have a Best Buy cash-back card that pays you 5 percent back per dollar spent, which in effect would net you $100 in cold hard cash for your purchase of the computer.

Given this scenario, why on earth *wouldn't* you buy it with that card, earn the cash-back credit, and enjoy your computer just the same? Does it cost you any extra money or time to do so? Not at all, particularly if you already have the cash on hand to pay off the next billing cycle in full. Remember, due to the revolving nature of the credit cycle, you get to enjoy a one-month lag time before you even need to make that payment, and more importantly, before they begin to charge you any interest. Furthermore, if you're lucky enough to be banking during a time when banks are paying high interest, you also just got to hold onto and keep earning interest on your money for that much longer.

Well, this is very similar to how IBC works for you. In essence, you finance everything that you purchase, running them through your own "rewards system" of personal banking—in and out—through your policy loans. As you pay back your policy loans (remember, since it's your own bank, why wouldn't you?), the equivalent loan interest and any additional PUA you can deposit only further serves to increase even faster your cash values and death benefit. In fact, the more you use it in this way, the better it gets.

After a few short years, every new dollar that you continue to put into your IBC policy (particularly the PUA) immediately purchases a generous multiple of that deposited value in increased death benefit for the long term. At the same time, these dollars also purchase and add more to your ever-growing cash value than the amount deposited at that time, for your immediate use and benefit. This is akin to a business finally becoming net profitable, the key difference being that this type of policy grows more and more profitable every year, guaranteed, unlike any business that I know of. Eventually, with enough size and/or policies, you will never need to use (or pay) another commercial bank again, whether it's for a new car, vacation, home improvement project, business, or college loan, or even another home or investment property.

When Walt Disney initially took hold of his dream and needed investment capital, the banks wouldn't lend to him. However, through a fortuitous policy loan out of his own IBC-styled whole life policy, he started the Disney Company and founded the iconic international amusement theme park empire. Colonel Sanders, of Kentucky Fried Chicken fame, did the same with his policy loan, peddling his original secret fried chicken recipe to every restaurant who would give him an audience, and finally opening his own first KFC restaurant. This, of course, developed into the multibillion-dollar franchise we all know and love today. Even the late US Senator, presidential candidate, and Vietnam War hero, the esteemed John McCain, funded his political campaigns using Infinite Banking and his family's policies. There is no shortage of famous and successful entrepreneurs who have harnessed the power of their IBC systems and changed the course of their destinies with it.

Families don't realize how much money they give up to the bank over a lifetime in the form of interest. An average American will spend roughly 34.5 percent interest on stuff we buy. This includes your car, house, education, vacation, medical bills, and just general living expenses. IBC not only allows you to stop paying for all this interest, but in fact turns this negative drag completely around *into your favor, by earning this interest instead of paying it!* Furthermore, the immediate death benefit supporting the policies of this system gives you and your family a peace of mind that they will be provided for at your "graduation" off this planet, in a simple, probate- and tax-free manner.

Chapter 10

USING IBC TO FINANCE A CAR PURCHASE: A CASE STUDY

When first learning about how the Infinite Banking Concept financial strategy works, a common question people ask is, "How can this work *practically* in my everyday life?" To demonstrate this and how effective IBC can be, let's walk through an example of a person purchasing vehicles over his lifetime. There's nothing magical or special about cars when it comes to IBC. Buying vehicles just happens to be something common to many of us—something we have experience in and will likely do many times over the course of our lives. A car purchase often requires financing or planning and is a fairly large purchase for most.

In the financial world, we are traditionally taught one of two ways to purchase a vehicle. We either pay cash or take out a loan from the bank or auto dealer. Both methods will net you a car; however, both also lead us to having zero dollars at the end of the deal. The graph below illustrates the difference of our cash flow's movement between these two most popular ways of purchasing a vehicle:

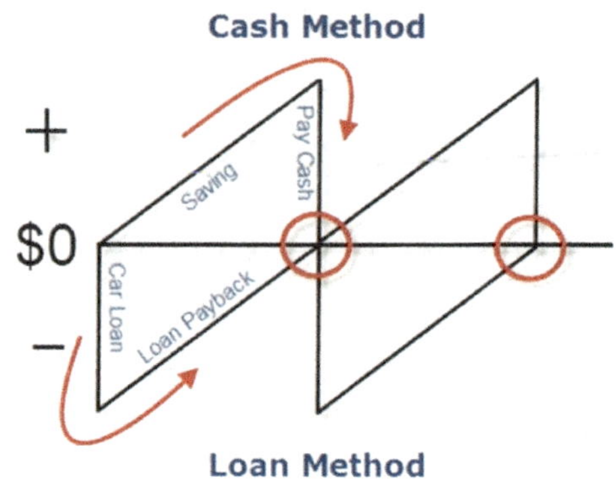

Look at this cash line example above. Follow the bottom arrow in the car loan method, where we take out a loan for the car and turn around to pay the cash in exchange for it. In this case, we are immediately in the negative and make scheduled payments toward the car loan to eventually get us back to the zero-balance center line. Oftentimes, once the car is paid off, we need or want to trade in and buy another car, and we start the process all over again.

The second option, following the top arrow, of using all cash is typically considered the better option because we can save money by not paying the interest charge. Here we'll often delay the purchase and steadily save up for some amount of time to build up our car fund. Once we have enough cash saved, we withdraw that whole amount and pay for the vehicle up front. Our savings is depleted to zero, and we typically must start saving again for the next car down the road.

Notice the red circles? Although they trend up or down periodically, both methods lead back to the same result: *the big fat zero-dollar line*. No continuing compounding interest or growth of any kind happens on our dollars with either method. Money just passes through our hands, either down and up or up and down, ever out the door, but never helps us build wealth. We either pay interest to someone else (loan method) or miss out on the interest we could have earned with our money (savings method). At the end of a lifetime of car purchases, the result is the same: $0.

IBC provides an alternative method for financing things we already spend money on by using an entity that we own and control. The foundational principle is that anytime we can cut out the interest we pay to others, by using our own asset, which is subject to minimal taxation, we will improve our wealth-generating potential significantly. This is made possible by following IBC's three core wealth-building principles:

1. We pay ourselves (by making deposits into our system).
2. We recapture lost dollars (interest coming back to us in our tax-favorable system).
3. We pay interest on our own dollars (charging market rate or higher for use of our dollars).

Using our car-buying example, IBC allows us to buy the same car and end up much further on the positive side of the cash line each time we buy a car. Let's see how this works using an example of a typical life insurance contract that's specially designed for

IBC. This policy is for a male, age thirty-five, with a preferred status. The annual premium deposit is $4,000 with an added paid-up addition (PUA) of $6,000 for the first four years. This PUA drops to the minimum $100 at year five and beyond to keep the option to continue to overfund into the future. This is the foundational design used by many IBC practitioners. We'll break it down later, but here is a high-level view:

Using IBC for Car Purchases

life success & legacy

Policy End of Year	Age	Premium Deposits	Car Purchases	Annual Car Loan Repayments	Cash Value	Net Death Benefit
1	36	$10,000			$5,881	$333,876
2	37	$10,000			$13,303	$360,473
3	38	$10,000			$23,555	$386,445
4	39	$10,000	$20,000	$4,800	$18,168	$395,444
5	40	$4,100		$4,800	$27,668	$401,129
6	41	$4,100		$4,800	$36,963	$407,354
7	42	$4,100		$4,800	$46,720	$414,090
8	43	$4,100		$4,800	$56,784	$426,774
Deposits *minus* Car Purchases *plus* Repayments:		$60,400		Total Cash Available in Your System:	$56,784	
9	44	$4,100	$20,000	$4,800	$46,339	$412,960
10	45	$4,100		$4,800	$56,341	$419,649
11	46	$4,100		$4,800	$67,323	$428,494
12	47	$4,100		$4,800	$78,894	$438,032
13	48	$4,100		$4,800	$90,918	$452,522
Cash Put In:		$84,900		Cash Available:	$90,918	
14	49	$4,100	$20,000	$4,800	$82,565	$441,754
15	50	$4,100		$4,800	$94,821	$451,493
16	51	$4,100		$4,800	$107,677	$461,669
17	52	$4,100		$4,800	$121,212	$472,468
18	53	$4,100		$4,800	$135,287	$487,243
Cash Put In:		$109,400		Cash Available:	$135,287	
19	54	$4,100	$20,000	$4,800	$129,101	$478,037
20	55	$4,100		$4,800	$143,637	$489,604
21	56	$4,100		$4,800	$158,716	$501,485
22	57	$4,100		$4,800	$174,362	$513,703
23	58	$4,100		[illegible]	[illegible]	[illegible]
Cash Put In:		$133,900		Cash Available:	$190,484	
24	59	$4,100	$20,000	$4,800	$186,413	$520,862
25	60	$4,100		$4,800	$203,132	$533,495
26	61	$4,100		$4,800	$220,592	$546,685
27	62	$4,100		$4,800	$238,866	$560,619
28	63	$4,100		$4,800	$257,799	$577,213
29	64	$4,100			$272,653	$587,645
30	65	$4,100			$288,118	$598,624
		$146,600 Total Deposits	$100,000 Total Car Purchases	$120,000 Total Repayments		

Policy Details
Male, Age 35, Preferred
Base: $4,000
PUA: $6,000; $100 min
Non-Guaranteed Assumptions
IRate: 4.76%

Car Loan Details
Amount: $20,000
Length: 5 years @ 7.42%
Monthly: $400
Annual: $4800

Deposits
- Car Purchases
+ Repayments

$166,600
Total Cash Outlay

This gentleman starts his IBC policy and chooses to capitalize it for four years, saving up for a vehicle just as he would have if he were using the cash method. Notice that by year three of this policy he has $23,555 of cash value available for him to use. In the fourth year, he goes to the dealership and buys a $20,000 car by borrowing against the cash value of his policy. Being an honest banker, and knowing he would normally have to pay interest to a lender to use that money, he charges himself interest and sets a monthly "car payment." He ends up with a fairly standard payment of $400 per month, which is a five-year note at 7.42 percent. He pays himself back into his policy (via his loan repayment) a total of $4,800 annually. Not only is his policy continuously growing, but the interest payments he is paying himself further contribute to the growth of the cash value.

Notice the $166,600 number in the lower right-hand corner? That is the total amount of money he used over thirty years to purchase his IBC policy, fund his system, and purchase five vehicles (including all repayments). However, at this point he is sixty-five years old and has access to a total of $288,118 in cash value. As a side benefit, he has almost $600,000 (and growing) in death benefit that will eventually pass on, tax free, to his family, church, or school, or a charity he cares about. Did he get the use of his five cars? *Yes!* Did he recover every single penny he used to buy these cars? *Yes!* Did he provide a sizable tax-free benefit to his heirs? *Yes!* He essentially got to use *his* dollar *multiple times!*

Let's take a closer look at the first section. He purchases a dividend-paying, whole life insurance asset that he pays for with

$4,000 per year in premium. For the first four years, he takes the option to put extra cash into his system, up to $6,000 per year, for a total of $10,000 per year. Starting in year five, he keeps this option in place for the minimum $100 per year, for a total annual premium of $4,100, which doesn't increase or change for the rest of the example.

Policy End of Year	Age	1 Premium Deposits	Car Purchases	Annual Car Loan Repayments	2 Cash Value	Net Death Benefit
1	36	$10,000			$5,881	$333,876
2	37	$10,000			$13,303	$360,473
3	38	$10,000		3	$23,555	$386,445
4	39	$10,000	$20,000	$4,800	$18,168	$395,444
5	40	$4,100		$4,800	$27,668	$401,129
6	41	$4,100	$4,100	$4,800	$36,963	$407,354
7	42	$4,100	+$4,800	$4,800	$46,720	$414,090
8	43	$4,100	$8,900	$4,800	$56,784	$426,774
Deposits *minus* Car Purchases *plus* Repayments:		$60,400	4	Total Cash Available in Your System:	$56,784	$10,064 5

If we look at the short term, we will see that he is eight years in and has almost broken even. In year eight, he has access to 94 percent ($56,784 / $60,400) of the money he put in. Why not 100 percent? The insurance company must be paid up front: it is a business, and people and processes behind the scenes make this system function. It's easy to forget that when starting a business or buying a cash-flowing asset, we put in money up front because it will be profitable in the long run.

Notice that in year eight, he puts in a total of $8,900 ($4,100 premium + $4,800 repayment). However, the cash value of the policy grew a total of $10,064 from year seven ($46,720) to year eight ($56,784). In other words, he made a deposit of less than $9,000 into his banking system, and more than $10,000 additionally was available for his use. This net-positive, year-over-year gearing actually starts in year three. Does the place where you currently store cash do that for you?

Continuing with the example in year nine, he takes his first car for trade-in with another $20,000 and goes down to the car lot and upgrades into a nicer, newer vehicle. He makes the same "car payments" back to his system over the next five years. Remember, this is no different than what he would be doing if he financed the car through the bank or dealership.

9	44	$4,100	$20,000	$4,800	$46,339	$412,960
10	45	$4,100		$4,800	$56,341	$419,649
11	46	$4,100		$4,800	$67,323	$428,494
12	47	$4,100	$4,100 +$4,800 $8,900	$4,800	$78,894	$438,032
13	48	$4,100		$4,800	$90,918	$452,522
	Cash Put In:	$84,900		Cash Available:	$90,918	$12,024

Now he is $6,000 ahead overall. In year thirteen, he puts in the same $8,900 but has an additional $12,024 available to use.

This trend continues for the next few car purchases. Since he borrows *against* his policy, using the asset as collateral rather than taking money *from* his system, he has not interrupted the compounding growth. This will pay off significantly the longer the policy is in effect. For this example, let's say he makes his last car purchase using this method at age fifty-nine.

24	59	$4,100	$20,000	$4,800	$186,413	$520,862
25	60	$4,100		$4,800	$203,132	$533,495
26	61	$4,100		$4,800	$220,592	$546,685
27	62	$4,100		$4,800	$238,866	$560,619
28	63	$4,100		1 $4,800	$257,799	$577,213
29	64	$4,100			$272,653	$587,645
30	65	$4,100	2 $15,465		$288,118	$598,624
		$146,600	$100,000	$120,000		
		Total Deposits	Total Car Purchases	Total Repayments		

Deposits
- Car Purchases
+ Repayments

3 $166,600
Total Cash Outlay

1. He makes his last car payments back to himself in year twenty-eight (age sixty-three). From then on, he only makes his annual premium deposit of $4,100.
2. From year twenty-nine to year thirty (age sixty-five), his cash value grew by **$15,465**.
3. Also at this point, he has put in a total of **$166,600**. This includes his premium deposits plus all repayments back into his system, minus the money he used to purchase cars. His available cash value to use is **$288,118**. Furthermore, he still enjoys **$598,624** in death benefit!

Simply by learning how to take control of the financing in his life on a purchase he was already going to make, he significantly changed his future. Into his seventies and eighties, the numbers just keep growing. So, too, does that death benefit, which he will pass on tax free to those he loves and cares about. In fact, he could start policies on his kids and grandkids and teach them how to finance their purchases, or even be the bank for the younger generation. Think about it, even in your own life. How quickly do twenty or thirty years go by?

Could he have done this with his wife's car and doubled the numbers? Could he be the banker for his child(ren)'s and grand-kids' cars, where they pay him those interest payments instead of the bank down the street? Vehicles are just one example of things we finance in life. This concept applies to anything for which we typically borrow money from a bank to purchase, including vacations, education, weddings, home purchases, renovations, investments, business equipment, etc. It is called the Infinite Banking Concept financial strategy because the possibilities are as big as your imagination! When set up and capitalized properly, these whole life policies, after so many years, can also serve to supplement and even in some cases provide for your retirement income.

Chapter 11

The Income Snowball . . . I'd Buy That for a Dollar!

What if someone told you that if you gave them a dollar, they would give you back your dollar *and* twenty cents? You might be interested in hearing more, wouldn't you? Now let's add that the original dollar you gave for the $1.20 wasn't even yours to begin with—you borrowed it for the short time necessary to buy the $1.20, and for just the price of a few cents in interest cost. How would that sound? Pretty cool, I would think, at least for anyone who can do simple math!

Finally, what if you could repeat this deal again and again, each time adding more and more of those profitable trades to your own bank? This example and thought exercise set the stage for the most powerful, income-producing, cash-flow-generation strategy known as the Income Snowball. With it, you can rapidly build up a cash-flowing asset that harnesses for you the most powerful forces of Velocity Banking that we explained in depth earlier.

The Income Snowball and the patented calculator used to

plan out and run this strategy is a revolutionary financial concept and tool invented by Tanisha Souza, JD, CEO and founder of Tardus Wealth Strategies. In essence, it is simply the process of borrowing money in the short term (thus at a low cost) and using it to purchase a long-term, amortized, and consequently profitable income-producing asset that pays you back over an extended time period. However, there's a special manner as to how you implement this process so that you can continue buying and building up more and more of this profitable future income that you end up layering, one on top of the other, to compound and grow over time.

The longer payback period of this income stream is crucial here, because what you do is stack these consecutive income-producing purchases one after the other. By laddering them to overlap in their start and end dates, you allow them to continuously compound until the very first "stack" or "flip" is completely paid out and finally ends, typically three years later. However, well before this ever happens, you will have purchased several more of these, having added to the original. In this manner, you will be making much more than you ever stop getting paid for at that time. Because of the effect of gaining momentum and compounding, your snowball's increasing growth will always remain profitably ahead of its slower decline and will continue growing at ever-increasing speed (and size). This is just like a snowball rolling down a mountain, gathering more and more snow, going faster and faster as it gets heavier and larger.

Naturally, the point of this ever increasing snowball is to be able to start pulling out enough passive money to live off of. But just when can this happen? And how much can I pull? At some point in the future, your snowball will be large enough to "peel off" a perpetual amount to pay for all your bills and expenses. According to Tardus, this is known as your "Financial Freedom Date" and with their patented calculator, your coach can determine this for you, given your particular income needs and current cash flow situation.

Note that two key metrics and relative dimensions are at play in this process. Of course, there's the cost of the interest rate of your borrowed money and the (hopefully higher) rate of gain or benefit from your purchased income money. There's also the much shorter length of time for the original money that you borrow to use (duration cost) and the longer duration of incoming money you earn and therefore benefit/gain from.

Naturally, common sense tells you that any cost should always be less than your benefit or gain, and therefore should net you a positive profit. For example, the rate (APY) you earn from the investment or income source ideally should be higher than the rate (APR) you pay to borrow the initial capital, and whenever possible, this is always preferable. However, one curious aspect about the Income Snowball is that even if this condition is not met, it's not necessarily a deal breaker. In fact, what's proven to be much more important is the nature of the interest paid and of the interest earned. In this case, it's interest paid from a short-term, declining balance in exchange for the profitable interest earned from an amortized, long-duration income stream. That time-period difference whereby you use the money for (short term) to buy the income with (long term or amortized) is what really makes the magic happen!

This differential gearing in both the interest rates (when

possible) in combination with the varying relative term periods (most important) is what really drives the overall profitability of the Income Snowball process. Note, however, that even if the rate you pay to borrow the money is the same as (or even slightly higher than) the rate you earn when you buy the future income stream, you will still come out ahead because of the importance of the *nature* of the interest earned versus what was paid.

For an extreme example, let's say that it costs you 10 percent (APR) to buy yourself a 5 percent (APY) income, which is a simple two-to-one *negative* ratio. On its face, this seems to be a pretty bum deal. However, let's also say that you use and *pay the 10 percent for only seven months*, while you get to *earn the 5 percent over thirty-six months*. Now, that difference in duration is just over a five-to-one positive ratio, right? This is a net gain in your favor that actually makes it worth the investment. How so?

Let's prove it with simple math. What did the seven months of money use cost you? If you borrowed $10,000 for a full year, that's simply $1,000. However, if you paid it all off at month seven, then that's just $583 (7/12 x $1,000). In reality, it's even less, since you typically pay it off in monthly installments, which continually decreases the remaining principal that the 10 percent interest rate is charged upon.

Now, what did that $10,000 at 5 percent APY earn you over three years? Remember that it's *amortized* just like a mortgage, but over thirty-six months, meaning that you are paid out in regular installments of about $300 per month, and that comes to $800.

If you subtract $583 from $800, that's a difference and profit of $217 that you earned from a modest 5 percent yielding, income-producing asset, all while paying 10 percent for the brief use of that $10,000. Bananas! This profit of $217 represents a *37 percent return* if you take it and divide it by the cost of your investment, or the $583 you paid in interest. And of course, if you can either borrow the money for the same rate (or lower) than you can earn on it, then this positive skew gets even better!

Chapter 12

Slow Your Roll: A Breakdown of the Snowball's Mechanics

Let's break this down more specifically with what is required to start your Income Snowball. First, you need to have a *positive cash-flow situation*. This just means that each month, after all of your regular expenses are paid out, you have some money left over with which you can reliably contribute to an investment—in this case, the snowball. A handy amount we can use for our example is a net positive $1,000 per month. This monthly contribution will help drive our snowball and what we will call our first "flip." However, we do not simply take our $1,000 and directly, or dollar for dollar, buy the income asset piecemeal every month. That would create a low-yield one-for-one exchange of your money that is simply too slow and misses out on the much higher potential income you could have by using the snowball method.

So, what do you do with this extra $1,000 per month? Understand that if you just saved it in your boring savings account at the bank for three years, you'd have just over $36,000 (plus some nominal interest of 0.01 percent). However, you'll see that we can do *much* better than that in this same thirty-six-month time period. Again, using the same principles of Velocity Banking let's dig in to how this works. Your first step is to open a line of credit (LOC) with your bank—heck, it could even be the same bank you already have your savings and checking accounts with. This LOC, however, has to be a *revolving, simple-interest debt instrument* from which you will draw money out of, for the *short term and at a low price.*

Let's assume you borrowed a nice round $10,000 from your LOC that has a 10 percent annual interest rate. With it, you immediately purchase your income stream that earns anywhere from 8–12 percent APY. This can be in the form of peer-to- peer (P2P) notes you buy from online debt consolidators such as Prosper. Such companies offer their customers a cheaper alternative to the banks to consolidate more expensive consumer debt, pay for medical bills, start a business, etc. In any event, just as with a bank, customers are graded according to their creditworthiness, taking into consideration their debt-to-income levels and credit scores. Generally speaking, the better the borrower is riskwise, the lower the rates they can get.

For example, Spendthrift Sally comes to Prosper with three high-interest credit card debts that average a whopping 25 percent. She wants to get rid of these and borrow from Prosper for the 20 percent rate she qualifies for to knock these out and save herself some money, which she can now use to buy that spring-essential Fendi bag! Prosper now owns this debt and, in turn, sells it (and thousands of other such notes) on the open market for investors like us to buy. Naturally, they take a cut of at least 1 percent for managing these notes; hence, investors buying these for income can expect anywhere from 6–8 percent for the best notes (in terms of lowest risk) all the way up to almost 20 percent for the riskiest borrowers, aka our now stylin'-for-spring Sally herself.

Since these are three-year notes, you are paid back all the interest and principal over a thirty-six-month time period. With a 12 percent annual APR, we can use our handy interest calculator from before to break this down, as illustrated below:

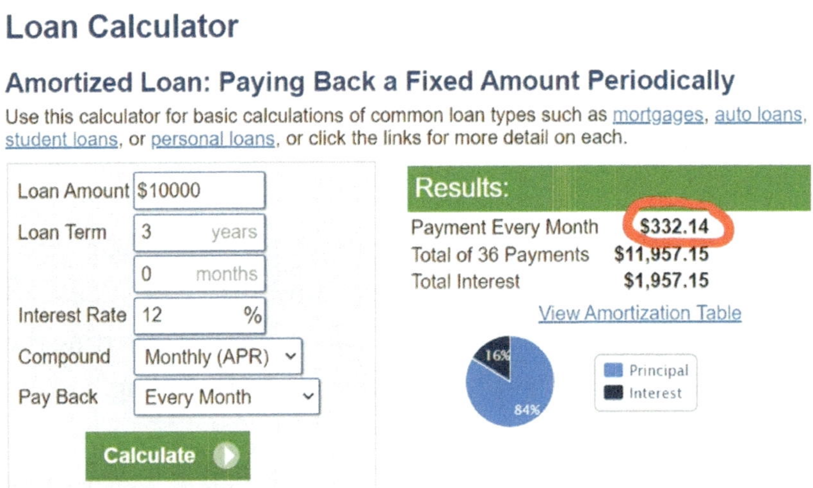

We see here that you can expect $332.14 per month for the next thirty-six months. Take this new income and add it to our present $1,000 cash-flow contribution, for a total of $1,332.14. This all goes right back to pay down our LOC. We do that this month, and every month afterward, until it's totally paid off. For this first time, it will take just 7.5 months. As soon as you pay off this initial $10,000 line of credit, you flip back and borrow it ($10,000) out again and buy another similar set of notes for the next "flip" of income stream.

Now, however, you have an extra $664.28 per month coming in from the two sets of performing notes (flips). Adding in your $1,000 contribution, you can use this $1,664.28 per month to pay down your line even faster, this time in just six months. Do you see a pattern here? With each completion of a flip, your speed increases. The momentum in your snowball is building, and eventually it's coming back so fast that it only takes between two to three months each time to pay off your $10,000 LOC.

What do you do at that point? Notice that as your speed increases to pay down your $10,000 LOC, each time the decrease in time slows down just a bit, to the point of it becoming an example of diminishing returns. To solve this, you simply increase your flip size! Just how much will depend on what your coach and Tardus's patented calculator determines. The time it takes to pay down your larger LOC will, of course, increase, resetting the time to pay it down, just like the first time, depending on how much larger you go up.

Remember, though, that you now also have much more coming back to you each month, even with the same monthly $1,000 contribution commitment. Also, since your flip size has increased or possibly even doubled, you are getting much more each month in passive income. You simply repeat the very same process monthly, speeding up your flips, until you have to go bigger, yet again. Sooner than you can imagine, your flip size (what you borrow out each time from the LOC) will be in the tens of thousands, and with all those flips layered on top of one another, your monthly payout will be running into the thousands! As a personal note, by our third year, we were at a $35,000 flip size, and bringing in around $12,000 per month, passively.

At this point, many of you may be thinking, what if I can't find these income-producing investments that can reliably return 8–12 percent per year? Don't fret. Remember that with Velocity Banking, *it's not the number as much as the nature of the debt or investment that really matters.* Rest assured you're only paying generally between three to seven months' worth of interest per flip or stack to earn the thirty-six months of future income and amortized interest. So even if your initial $10,000 investment or note loaned out earns just 5 percent APY with which you start to stack your income, you're actually quite okay. In fact, even the rest of your subsequent stacks could be that low, and as long as they pay out steadily for the thirty-six months, you'll still be fine.

Take a look at the simple example below, which my wife, Pei-Jiin, first came up with to provide a "proof of concept" that the numbers and mechanism of the snowball really work. Remember that we were both teachers in the not-so-distant past and therefore still had a roll of butcher paper that we used to draw out what I now consider to be the coolest mathematical word problem ever! Basically, after borrowing $10,000, you lend it out each time to a trusted family member or friend, whom you charge a low interest rate of just 5 percent APR over three years. The works out to just $800 per $10,000 (see the loan calculator example from the last chapter). That's right, follow the numbers below and see how, within three years, you will have been able to buy over $75,600 worth of income—that is, stacked and flipped the $10,000 LOC seven times—all with the very same $1,000 monthly contribution.

Step 1: Borrow $10,000 from an LOC @ 10 percent APR. Lend it to Borrower A @ 5 percent APR.

This pays you $300 per month for thirty-six months. Adding this to your $1,000 monthly contribution = **$1,300**/month. Paying it all back to your LOC, it takes **7.7 months** to pay off your first flip.

Step 2: Borrow $10,000 from the same LOC and lend to Borrower B for the additional $300. Now you have **$1,600**/month going to pay down your LOC (2 x $300 + $1,000), and it takes **6.25 months** to pay off.

Step 3: Borrow $10,000 and lend it out again for the additional $300. Now you have a total of **$1,900**/month paying down your LOC, which takes **5.26 months** to pay off.

Step 4: Borrow $10,000 and lend again for a now **$2,200** monthly payment, which will pay down the LOC in **Step 4** in only **4.5 months.**

Step 5: Borrow the same $10,000 again, lend again, and return **$2,500**/month to the LOC, paying it down in just **4 months**.

Step 6: Borrow $10,000 again for **$2,800**/month. Now we're really cooking, and we pay off this LOC in **3.6 months**.

Step 7: Borrow $10,000 for the now **$3,100**/month that goes back in, and your final flip here takes just **3.2 months**. Can you see the pattern here? Faster and faster your flips will come.

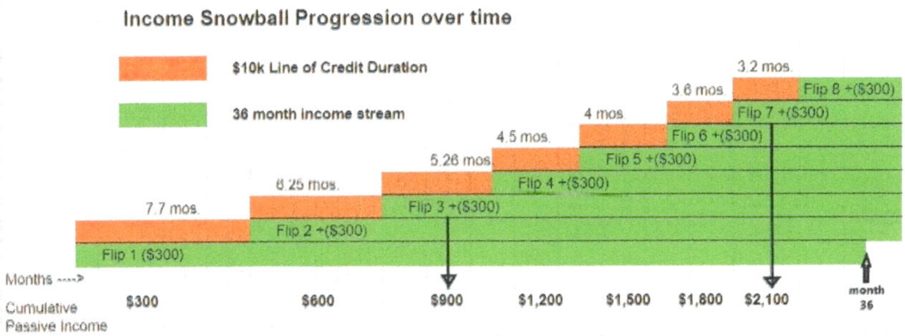

Pausing here, at this point you're closing in at thirty-six months and have been able to lend out/invest your $10,000 a whopping *seven* times, all with the same LOC! With a total of $75,600 in conservative, low-interest loans all returning money back to you, you've essentially built yourself that income. (Note though, that a majority of this income, both principal and interest, has already been paid back to you, ever since the first flip's first monthly payment). Your snowball pays you every month, with the last few paying you $2,100, and all of it passively! Consider that if you had charged more interest, used a cheaper funding source, or earned a few percent more in an investment fund, the numbers would only be better.

Note here, though, that after month thirty-six, the very first loan or investment is paid out in full, so that flip's $300 monthly income ends, but we also have more money coming in now to replace it, significantly overcompensating for that periodic slippage. At year three, with over $2,000 per month of *passive* money incoming, if you simply keep your flips going, the snowball continues to grow, faster and faster, bigger and bigger.

We just saw how we built that income stream, but what did it cost us? After all, we did use OPM and were charged for it, right? Absolutely, and to recap what it cost for us to build the $75,600 snowball, we invested into it our own money of $1,000 per month for the thirty-six months, or $36,000. Additionally, we paid some interest for the use of the bank's money—via the 10 percent LOC—for leverage to buy all that income. Assuming we used that money for the full twelve months per year, for all three years at the 10 percent rate (which, by the way, we never came close to, since we paid it down again and again over that time frame), that amounts to a maximum cost of $3,000. Add this to the $36,000 of our own money we put into it, and that's a total maximum all-in cost to you of $39,000.

But remember, we did seven flips total, resulting in the $75,600 of a steady, income-producing asset! Even with such a low-yielding investment and relatively high cost of capital, this example mathematically proves that the chronologically differential gearing of the flips is much more important than the nominal interest rate that you can earn. The true power of DIBS is the Income Snowball employing Velocity Banking principles at full force and getting multiple uses of that same $10,000 within the three years. This is the real key to this amazing process. Doing so many times significantly compounded the profitability of your 5 percent yielding flips over the three years.

On a final note, consider this fun fact: as soon as we have our IBC system set up and running, we actually *have our own bank* that we *fully control* and can use on our own terms, rather than depending on a commercial one that can (and often do!) change its rates or repayment schedules at will. Furthermore, because it's our own line of credit, specifically from the cash values as a policy loan, the interest that would normally exit our personal monetary system instead returns right back into our system via the annual dividend that grows our policy each and every year!

Over the years we have tried all sorts of different income-producing assets for our own snowball. We personally have found this to be the very best means to run our Income Snowball, completely within our IBC system of policies. This was the genesis, evolution, and ultimately highest-level application of the Dynamic Income Banking System, and it has made all the difference for us. The seamless combination and integration of IBC and the Income Snowball is what it truly means to have DIBS *on your money*, to put it all to work so it can grow and thrive, as we'll see in the next chapter.

Chapter 13

DIBS - The Ultimate Combination - Running Income Snowball within Your IBC System

What do a PBJ (peanut butter and jelly) sandwich and a Reese's Peanut Butter Cup have in common? Both are favorite sweet treats, indeed, but both are also the magnificent results of combining two otherwise mundane ingredients, jelly and chocolate, to a common one: peanut butter! The PBJ sandwich is just two slices of bread, with jelly spread on one and peanut butter on the other, but smacking said slices together magically produces a tasty sandwich. The Reese's Cup is essentially that same peanut butter, but here ingeniously encased within a sweet chocolate shell sitting in a paper cup, resulting in the iconic candy that we all know and love today.

The IBC and the Income Snowball are also a match made in heaven. Each on its own is an amazing financial concept and practice that, when done properly, will greatly improve your financial trajectory in short order as well as permanently. Setting up your IBC policies to run your own banking system allows you to finance everything you purchase or invest in. These dividend-paying whole life policies are the ultimate permanent asset and even can set up your retirement and legacy for your next generation. And running your Income Snowball rapidly provides you a steady, increasing, passive-income stream that will financially free you from the rat race and the 40/40/40 "American Nightmare." However, when you do *both* and effectively *run them together* in a synergistic way, it blows the roof off what each can accomplish on its own, impressive as that is.

It's easy to understand why and how we would replace a commercial bank's line of credit with our own IBC bank's policy loan from our existing and available cash value. You save on interest and control that side of the snowball equation for the obvious benefits. However, the ultimate epiphany occurred when we realized that the very best asset to invest into on the other side of that equation was right under our noses! Remember how the snowball works even if we charge next to nothing on our flips? And that it's so much better when we can charge and earn more? The key to it was in the regular thirty-six months of payment back into our snowball. As long as you can reliably count on that repayment schedule, it works!

So guess who is the very best and safest borrower/payer of debt? The person I can always count on to pay, especially if that payment will reap me profits when done like clockwork? Like the late King of Pop, Michael Jackson, sings in his "Man in the Mirror,"

> I'm starting with the man in the mirror (oh)
> I'm asking him to change his ways (oh)

That's right, folks, that ideal borrower is *me*! And I will "make that change" and swap out the commercial bank with my own IBC "policy A" to take control and ownership of the funding side of the snowball equation. On the other side of it, I will simply swap out the potentially risky investment portfolio or P2P notes of anonymous borrowers online with my very own debt that I may already have in my IBC "policy B"!

This second part is where most people stop and scratch their heads. But think of this . . . What does the investment firm or P2P company do when you put your money with it or, in effect, buy your future stream of income? Simply put, it *invests* it into the speculative stock market or depends on anonymous borrowers like Spendthrift Sally. And what does your mutual, dividend-paying, whole life insurance company do with your money that's put into your policy and the company, whether as premiums or loan payments? The very same thing: it *invests* it, typically in much safer bonds or real estate-backed assets, from the premiums paid into the insured pool of capital covering the death benefits of all policyholders.

Both companies invest your money to be profitable—and in that sense they are similar—but in different ways, with the investment firms/P2P company being much riskier than the mutual insurance company. Bear in mind that the investment firms and P2P companies are both just a few years or decades old, whereas our mutual insurance company is well over a century old, with an astounding record of consecutive dividends paid each and every year and much more secure investments to boot.

Furthermore, does that investment firm or P2P company pay you any dividend at the end of the year? *No.* Do you have any control over the payment schedule or any guarantees built into their investment of your money? Also *no*. But your IBC policies, along with the contractual built-in guarantees, do pay annual dividends, and *you fully control* your payment schedule. Simply put, you decide your own ideal repaid interest rate! All it takes is for you to pay yourself back each month in the form of a policy loan from policy B. Remember that with IBC, we never withdraw from your policy, and our policy's cash value growth will never be interrupted. Add this amount—whether it's $300, $330, or $350 (your choice!)—to your monthly contribution, and together the total goes right back to pay down policy A's loan, just as we did before.

For example, our low-interest loans paid out just $300 monthly per $10,000 invested. In reality, you can adjust that to whatever you please, and it can work even better than our original instructive case. If you want faster-burning fuel for your snowball, you can ramp it up to, say, $340 per month by using your other IBC policy as the investment. Or if you'd like, you can even tamp it down to feel safer, as it may then even exceed the thirty-six-month expected schedule. A good coach can help you determine the ideal monthly amount given your particular goals. The important thing is that, because you own and benefit on both sides of this snowball equation with your IBC system of policies, you are in complete control and can, in effect, play both sides and win-win-win all around.

Chapter 14

CONCLUSION

The Dynamic Income Banking System (DIBS) is the powerful systematic combination of two amazing financial strategies that allows you to set up your private bank, finance everything you buy or invest in, and run your Income Snowball to build increasing passive cash flow for even more profit. Each system—the Infinite Banking Concept financial strategy and the Income Snowball—when done separately will benefit you and markedly improve your financial well-being. However, through DIBS, this powerfully efficient combination of two systems properly set up and working together will provide you a rock-solid and secure house of wealth and prosperity from which you will operate your income-generating money machine, building increasing monthly cash flow and guaranteed, tax-advantaged growth.

So what specific steps do you need to take? With so much information shared in this book, just where should you start? In my opinion, all we really know for sure is that we will all "graduate off this earth" and eventually kick the proverbial bucket. We also now know that IBC immediately sets up a secure and tax-free death benefit for loved ones, such as my wife and daughter, in that imminent event. For this personal reason, setting up my whole life policies was the most important place to start—as we did nine years ago when I was still on active duty in the Navy—especially since they can take some time to capitalize and become fully efficient. Think about it: you won't be any younger or (typically) much healthier than you are today.

Additionally, when set up properly for IBC purposes, your money goes right to work in three key ways. First, your premium deposit immediately supports the significant death benefit from the company's huge pool of capital, instantly providing your family, loved ones, or even your business with financial protection should you meet your maker unexpectedly. Second, your money in the policy begins its uninterrupted, compounding growth, just like our car purchase example. Third, a majority of your money, even your first year in and increasingly so in subsequent years, is *immediately available for you to use or invest again*, through the policy loans that are collateralized from your cash values. This third use of your dollars is such a game changer that many lose sight of the tremendous advantage it really is.

Think about it. Let's say that your typical return on investment earns around 8 percent. That sounds pretty good, but consider that while everyone else only profits from that once, with the IBC you can use those same dollars and put them to work, again and again, in multiple assets and investments over time. Your hard-working dollars from your own IBC private banking system may grow in cash values at a safe and humble 4 percent on the initial go (tax-free, I should add), but when used and reused (or invested and reinvested) three or four times, your money soon yields very robust, double-digit returns! All because your compounding growth within your policy(ies) is (are) never interrupted.

Next, get started on your Income Snowball. Remember how

we used an LOC from a commercial bank to start and run your Income Snowball? That works just fine, but if you already have a capitalized IBC policy, the smarter route would be to use your cash value, which is revolving and liquid, just like an LOC but from *your own bank*. Instead of paying the 10 percent to the commercial bank, you often can enjoy a lower 5 percent (or less) rate, where the interest goes back to a company *that you own*, as a mutual policyholder. Also, since no outside bank has control over your IBC LOC, it cannot reduce your limit or close them, as I have seen happen, even to our own LOCs. In fact, your IBC cash values not only will never go away, but they will also grow each year, guaranteed! Thus, having your IBC system set up first is a tremendous advantage for the snowball—and really for any investment you decide upon.

Furthermore, let's say you have another capitalized IBC policy B, particularly one with a "hole" such as an existing policy loan out from its cash values, that you can "fill in" and repay. Essentially, you can *buy out your own debt* in this second policy (with money from your first policy) and *structure monthly payments back out, to yourself*, specifically right back to your original funding source, policy A. The money basically just goes back and forth in a time-staggered fashion, just as the snowball intends, but now runs completely within your IBC system, perpetually growing both of your policies and your snowball.

It clearly pays to have one IBC policy, but it pays even more when you have two! Remember, you control the terms of that policy cash value loan and, consequently in this case, the payback schedule as you see fit. If you merely emulate the same regular thirty-six-month payments as you had with an outside borrower, the snowball doesn't care whom it's from and will work just the same. You are in control of *both* sides of this snowball equation: the funding side (from the IBC LOC) and the income side (from your own IBC debt that you purchased and will pay back). Just imagine if that debt was used to invest in something else that also positively cash flows, like an entirely secondary source of passive income!

In fact, we now can use our snowball income (for just one month at a time) to open entirely new policies, and without even requiring a dollar of any new money. We're essentially just recycling our money to make more "pots of gold" or branches of our bank! It's a tremendous strategy that allows us to "franchise" more policies and expand our growing IBC system, which of course serves to perpetuate our ever-growing Income Snowball. The synergy here is truly astounding and like nothing else I've ever seen or experienced. It's almost as if the two strategies were made for each other.

To get started with IBC, visit my friends and colleagues over at Life Success & Legacy (www.lifesuccesslegacy.com), where you can watch numerous videos and podcasts, sign up for a free online IBC webinar, and even set up a one-on-one coaching session. Founders Mike Everett and Chris Bay helped us set up many more policies for the Kwong family banking system. Mike is an originator, or OG, and personal student and friend of the late, great man himself, Nelson Nash. Mike and his team practice IBC in the purest sense, adhering to the fundamental values of IBC that Nelson preached. Chris is a former public school principal, a lifelong educator, and a naturally patient and clear presenter and coach of the concept. They firmly believe in empowering clients with education and offer personalized guidance and targeted plans customized for your own financial situation.

To get started with your Income Snowball you should check out Tanisha and Chris Souza's team over at Tardus (www.Tardus.com). That's exactly where we started ourselves. There you'll find a treasure trove of information about the Income Snowball and can also contact someone who will tell you more about their system and how their coaching works. Their website is also packed with great videos visually explaining how the system works, and you can set up your free coaching call with a wealth coach.

Alas, this is the end of my book, but I hope only the beginning of your own journey. Remember the major themes we discussed. First, educate yourself and change your attitude toward money to that of abundance rather than scarcity. Focus on the present, cash-flowing potential of it to work for you, instead of always just working for it. Finally, never stop learning and improving with these strategies or discovering new ones, and always share with those near and dear to you. Your money is now truly alive, flowing and recirculating at an increasing pace and profitability that is limited only by your own imagination. I hope and trust that you will take action and command of your financial future. Get DIBS on your money, get off the hamster wheel, and mind your own chicken coop. May you have good luck, great health, and more wealth—and always keep it flowing forward and up!

ABOUT THE AUTHOR

Mike Kwong is the quintessential lifelong learner. After graduating from Brown University, he started off as a fashion retail executive in Boston, Massachusetts, where he met his brilliant and supportive wife and partner in all things, Pei-Jiin. There they bought their first of many investment properties over the years. After law school, Mike joined the Navy to learn Chinese and earned an associate degree. While stationed in Hawaii and working as an intelligence analyst for the National Security Agency, he started selling options on his dividend-paying stocks, always looking for new and better ways to earn extra, passive income. While still in active duty, he earned his MBA and also learned of the Infinite Banking Concept financial strategy, which allows one to set up their own private banking system. He was hooked and started policies for each member of his family.

After separating from the Navy and moving to Texas, Mike earned his master's degree in education and taught in public schools. The Kwongs eventually ran their own college consulting business, all while continuing to manage their stock and real estate portfolios. It was then that they learned of Tardus and the Income Snowball system. Soon enough, Mike and Pei-Jiin developed their Dynamic Income Banking System (DIBS) system, which seamlessly combines the two strategies of guaranteed, tax-free growth and compounding, passive income. Fine-tuning and mastering DIBS allowed them to become job-optional by forty-five and for Mike to pursue his life's ambition as a student-teacher. Now, he helps others reach financial freedom and make their money work for them, and he aims to share this system with the world, beginning with this book. Presently, Mike and Pei-Jiin live in Texas with their daughter, Jackie, and their two cats.

Made in the USA
Las Vegas, NV
02 November 2024

10929366R10056